LIFE IN
TUDOR PALACES
AND HOUSES

FROM 1485 TO 1603

ALISON SIM

IMPORTANT DATES

1485 Henry VII becomes king.

1503 James IV of Scotland marries Princess Margaret (Henry VIII's sister).

1509 Henry VII dies; Henry VIII becomes king.

1513 James IV defeated and killed at Battle of Flodden.

1520 Meeting between Henry VIII and Francis I of France at the Field of Cloth of Gold.

1527 Henry VIII appeals to the Pope to annul his marriage to Catherine of Aragon.

1533 Henry VIII marries Anne Boleyn.

1534 Act of Supremacy makes Henry VIII head of the Church of England.

1536 Anne Boleyn executed; Henry VIII marries Jane Seymour. Dissolution of the Monasteries begins.

1537 Prince Edward born; Jane Seymour dies in childbirth.

1540 Henry VIII marries Anne of Cleves, but quickly divorces her to marry Catherine Howard.

1542 Catherine Howard executed.

1543 Henry VIII marries Catherine Parr.

1545 *Mary Rose* sinks.

1547 Henry VIII dies; Edward VI becomes king.

1553 Edward VI dies; Lady Jane Grey becomes queen, but is replaced nine days later by Mary I.

1554 Wyatt's Rebellion, sparked by Mary I's intention to marry Philip of Spain; Mary I marries Philip of Spain; Lady Jane Grey beheaded.

1558 Calais, the last of the English possessions in France, is lost

1558 Elizabeth I becomes queen.

1569 Revolt of the Northern Earls, trying to replace Elizabeth with Mary, Queen of Scots as ruler of England.

1587 Mary, Queen of Scots executed.

1588 Defeat of the Spanish Armada.

1603 Elizabeth I dies.

➤ A reconstruction of the Saintlowe Tower at Kenilworth Castle, Warwickshire, in its Tudor heyday.

THE TUDOR PEOPLE

The Tudor period is one which feels remarkably familiar to many of us. The striking portraits of Henry VIII, Elizabeth I and their courtiers make a lasting impression. But what of the everyday lives of the Tudor people? What was it like to live in a noble household? After all, the courtiers' extravagant lifestyle required an army of people to maintain it, with large numbers employed in a wide variety of jobs, from private secretary to washerwoman. How did so many people live together without life turning into chaos? More specifically, how did the washerwomen keep the clothes clean? And how did you manage the catering if Queen Elizabeth I decided to come and stay?

Courtiers were, of course, exceptionally rich and influential people, and were no more typical members of their society than Hollywood stars are today, so if we are to understand the lives of more ordinary Tudors it helps to know the practicalities that lay behind their lives, too.

In an age of expanding trade, English merchants frequently spoke several languages and travelled a great deal in Europe. Their wives were often left at home, with considerable responsibilities. The everyday lives of these people reveal a self-confident class who felt quite at ease mingling with the aristocracy.

But ordinary Tudors had skills, too. Although most lacked academic education, this does not mean they were unintelligent. Even a ploughman, so often a figure of fun to the wealthy at the time, could generally perform a huge range of practical tasks on a farm. Housewives, too, might have little or no schooling, but were able to cook under Tudor conditions, as well as brew beer, work a dairy, look after animals, see to the medical needs of a family and servants – all whilst bringing up their families. The incredible amount of hard work and ingenuity that went into the ordinary tasks of daily life certainly makes us appreciate the possibilities of modern life.

NOBLE HOUSEHOLDS

Large households were not simply a luxury to the great – they were a vital demonstration of wealth and power. In Henry VIII's reign the Earl of Northumberland employed 166 people, and when Elizabeth I was queen William Cecil, as Baron Burghley, employed around 120. Although large numbers of servants were employed to do necessary jobs such as cooking, there were also well-educated administrative servants who looked after the many business interests of, and were gentlemen companions to, the masters they served. Virtually all live-in servants were male, except for ladies' attendants. Lady Margaret Long of Hengrave Hall in Suffolk employed five maids for herself and her daughters between 1541 and 1564. Women laundresses were also employed but they usually lived outside the household.

Great houses were good places to work as they provided security and opportunities for advancement. Allan King, from a local gentry family, started as a bailiff on one of the Earl of Northumberland's manors in 1581 and was steward of the household by 1592. Some servants went on to be employed in royal service. Sir John Daccombe became Chancellor of the Duchy of Lancaster after working for the Earl of Salisbury. Even the lower servants could do well: William Wistowe and William Chomeley climbed from obscurity to the highest office in the household of Edward Stafford, 3rd Duke of Buckingham.

⋏ William Cecil, 1st Baron Burghley, who had Burghley House in Lincolnshire built. Cecil was right-hand man to Elizabeth I.

Grand houses were run with regard to strict etiquette and worked a filter system of sorts. The surviving Tudor rooms at Hampton Court Palace show how the system worked. Many visitors were allowed into the first room, the large and impressive Great Hall. The aristocracy were allowed to progress through into the next room, the smaller Great Watching Chamber. Access from there to the king's private rooms was very strictly controlled, open only to those who worked there, and those whom the king wished to see. A similar system even existed inside the king's apartments.

Lords' lives revolved around ceremony. Publications such as John Russell's *Boke of Nurture*

◄ This painting of Haddon Hall in Derbyshire, by Laslett John Pott, demonstrates wealthy Elizabethan tastes in interior design.

INGATESTONE HALL

Ingatestone Hall in Essex was the home of William Petre, Secretary of State under Henry VIII. Great lords' houses were busy places which functioned like hotels, providing accommodation for the rich and powerful, and their servants. Petre's household accounts show that he entertained a constant stream of visitors here, from Princess Mary and various courtiers to craftsmen who came to work for the family. He had a household of around 40 people in the late 1540s and 1550s but his guests often outnumbered staff. In 1551–52 there was an average of 40 visitors at meals in winter and 80 in summer and autumn, when travelling was easier.

▼ Ingatestone Hall, home to the Petre family since the 16th century.

describe how there were ceremonies for all times of the day, from getting an aristocrat up and dressed to putting him to bed. The most effort was lavished on dinner, the main meal of the day, which was eaten around 12 noon–1 p.m. Russell describes how the preparation began with the formal laying of the lord's tablecloths and setting the tables, and ended with the lord's withdrawal to his private rooms at the end of the meal. Dinner took around two hours, so it is no surprise that lords ate their supper, their evening meal, in relaxed privacy. As the 16th century progressed, public dining became less common for great lords in their own homes but was still maintained by monarchs as a way of showing themselves to the court.

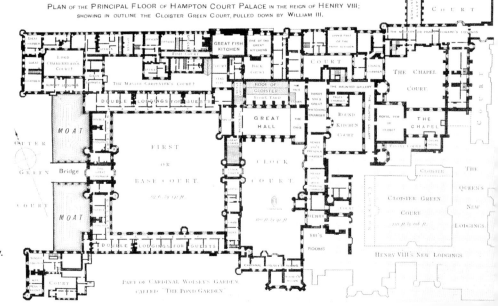

➤ Floor plan of Hampton Court Palace as it would have been during Henry VIII's reign. Access to the most prestigious rooms was only for the chosen few.

Merchants were important traders with overseas interests. They belonged to trade guilds which had considerable power, both locally and nationally. Even the City of London was run by the most important of the city's guilds. Merchants were well-educated men: a successful merchant needed more than just the ability to read and write. A knowledge of languages was useful and a good all-round education helpful for men who needed to move in European circles as part of their work. For example, John Johnson of Glapthorne Manor in Northamptonshire was a merchant at the Wool Staple – based across the English Channel in Calais – that controlled the export of wool. He could read and write fluently in French and Flemish, and had a good knowledge of Latin, which was at the time spoken by gentlemen across Europe. It was for this reason that the merchant class founded and supported a number of schools across the country, including St Paul's School in London, founded by The Mercers' Company in 1509.

There was not the great gulf between trade and the court that might be imagined. All powerful Tudors needed court connections and the merchants were no different. Anthony Cave – a merchant to whom John Johnson had once been apprenticed – had a brother who was a diplomat, and had family connections that included such

A   Sir Thomas Gresham (1519–79) was an extremely successful London mercer. He became Elizabeth I's agent in the Netherlands, and was founder of both the Royal Exchange and Gresham College in London.

important 'court' families as the Walsinghams of Scadbury Park in Kent, the Throckmortons of Coughton Court in Warwickshire and the Cecils of Hatfield House in Hertfordshire. Many of the 'new men' of Henry VIII's court, such as Thomas Cromwell, had a strong background in trade.

Merchants' wives and daughters were not simply social ornaments. They were reasonably well educated and could be left in charge whilst their husbands or fathers were away on business. The letters of the Johnson family show

◀   Built to impress: Paycocke's in Coggeshall, Essex, now in the care of the National Trust. The house dates from c.1500 and was built by John Paycocke, a wealthy wool merchant. The elaborately carved façade would have been painted in bright colours.

The Wynn Bed from Gwydir Castle in Wales. Carved beds like this were an important status symbol to the Tudors.

the women as capable individuals who dealt with everything from running the household to organizing the annual sheep shearing and the subsequent packing of the wool. If John Johnson's wife, Sabine, was typical of her day, it also shows the women of merchant families as being quite happy to argue with their husbands and make demands of them. Women were not allowed to set up as guild members independently but some did continue to run their husband's businesses if left a widow, so many must have known their spouse's line of work well.

Glapthorne Manor reflected John Johnson's status. The house had a panelled parlour and several rooms decorated with brightly painted linen cloths. John and Sabine slept in a fine wooden bed that John had commissioned in London and they owned at least two others. They enjoyed a lifestyle that was the equal of gentry families. The couple dressed well, their accounts recording the purchase of fine-quality

linen, wools and even some silks. When at table they enjoyed luxuries including a set of six silver goblets which had cost over £11 – a huge sum at the time. They were able to afford imported goods such as sugar, oranges and dried fruit. Their richer friend, Anthony Cave, bought in luxuries such as pepper, cloves, nutmeg, ginger and cinnamon in large quantities for Christmas celebrations.

The Johnsons' house was often full of guests: friends, family and business acquaintances. But their home life also showed an aspect of Tudor living that seems strange to us: although the Johnson children were much loved, they spent a great deal of time away from home. As babies they were sent to live with wet-nurses until the age of two or three. Even when they returned to live at home, the youngsters were often sent away on long visits to friends and relatives. Wealthy Tudors did not see the need to spend much time with their children – and the wealthier the family, the less the children saw of their parents.

➤ Tudor Merchant's House, Tenby in Pembrokeshire. Making a feature of the staircase was a way of showing that you were rising in the world.

ORDINARY HOUSEHOLDS

England was a mostly rural country in Tudor times; only about a fifth of the population lived in towns. Land was the safest investment and provided social prestige, so even those with no direct interest in agriculture bought land and built themselves country houses or further developed existing ones, like Sir William Cordell, a successful lawyer, who improved Melford Hall in Suffolk. For those lower down the social scale there was plenty of work in the countryside. Agriculture was labour-intensive and many industries depended on individuals working at home. Carding and spinning wool helped poorer families make ends meet, as did local enterprises, such as glove-making in Dorset and rush mat-making in Cornwall.

Life in the country was no rural idyll. Estimates suggest that between a third and a quarter of the entire rural population were farm labourers. These people were at the bottom of the agricultural hierarchy, as they were employed by the day and did the most strenuous and less prestigious work, such as digging ditches. Some labourers were fortunate enough to have a small plot of land on which to grow some food, but many had none at all.

Housing conditions for labourers varied considerably depending in which part of the country they lived. Of those labourers' cottages that are recorded, those in the north-west of England and the Welsh Marches tended to have only one room. In Cornwall, conditions were worse. In his *Survey of Cornwall,* published in 1602, Richard Carew describes older cottages with low thatched roofs and earth walls with a simple hole to let out the smoke from the fire. In wealthier Hertfordshire, such poverty was unusual. Here most cottages had a living room (known as the hall) with a chamber at one end or above. A buttery could often be found off the hall and some larger cottages had a milkhouse or dairy.

Most cottages were heated with one central fire, used for both warmth and cooking to save fuel. Beaten earth floors, which raised the dust, were common. Glass was falling in price but was still too expensive for most people. The 16th century was a period of inflation and labourers who had no land and relied on wages were hit hard. Their chances of modernizing their cottages, or of landlords paying for such improvements, were minimal.

Further up the ladder came the husbandmen and yeomen who farmed on a large enough scale to have produce to sell. They flourished as the growing population were eager customers for the food they produced. They often lived in

◄ Bayleaf Farmhouse has been moved from Chiddingstone in Kent to the Weald and Downland Open Air Museum in West Sussex. This is an example of an open hall house, which had gone out of fashion by the end of the 16th century.

➤ Bayleaf Farmhouse: a prosperous farmer's bedroom, furnished as it would have been in the early 15th century.

hall houses, consisting of a central hall which was open to the roof, with service rooms for storing food and cooking equipment at one end. At the other end would be the solar, the family's private bedroom and sitting room, with a parlour underneath. The parlour might be a more private room for the family or it could be used for working, storage and sleeping. These families could afford improvements – for example, replacing earth floors with brick or stone, and perhaps adding an upper floor to the hall, so that it was divided into living space below and bedchambers above. By the end of the 16th century, the old central hearth was often replaced with a chimney and fireplaces. This meant that one room could become a dedicated kitchen and, at last, the cooking equipment could be moved out of the living space. New houses were built with two storeys, without a hall. Some people at this level of society were rich enough to consider luxuries like glass windows and perhaps even a timber-framed staircase.

WEALDEN HALL HOUSE

Alfriston Clergy House in East Sussex is an example of a Wealden hall house – the name given to a typical timber-framed yeoman farmer's home, most common in the densely forested counties of East Sussex and Kent. Prosperous merchants and craftsmen often built similar houses in towns. This particular example may have been built as early as 1350 but such houses were still being built in the 16th century.

◄ The thatched Alfriston Clergy House, the first property acquired by the National Trust.

Grand households employed not only servants to clean and cook but also servants of honour. These were gentlemen of good education whose job it was to be the lord's companions and provide elegant set-dressing around the house. A servant of honour was expected to be involved in whatever pastime his master chose, whether it was hunting, gambling, dallying with mistresses or taking part in philosophical debate. Henry Percy, 9th Earl of Northumberland wrote some advice for his son, warning that he himself had chosen gentleman attendants whose expensive tastes had led him astray as a young man and so caused him to become heavily in debt. He told his son to chose his attendants with care.

Another role of these gentlemen was to take part in the ceremonial life of the household. There was a complicated etiquette to be observed when attending their masters. It was their job to observe this protocol and to deal with the many visitors that came to a great house with suitable tact, charm and deference. In an age when display was a vital part of maintaining political power, this was an important function.

The most trusted servants of honour had considerable responsibility. They might act as the steward who ran the household, or they might be

▲ A painting by Van Dyck of Henry Percy, 9th Earl of Northumberland (1564–1632), who claimed to have been led astray by his gentleman attendants.

responsible for collecting rents. Others might have an equally important but less definable role, such as John Husee who worked for Lord Lisle, Governor of Calais in the reign of Henry VIII. Husee acted as Lord Lisle's eyes and ears at court, keeping him informed of such vital information as who was in or out of royal favour. He was sent on errands to buy

◄ Four gentlemen – thought to be Sir Francis Walsingham, William Cecil, Lord Hunsdon and Sir Walter Raleigh – playing the card game primero. The painting shows the more intimate side of court life and the type of pastime that a servant of honour would have been expected to attend alongside his master.

CAST FROM COURT

In 1562 Queen Elizabeth I almost died from smallpox; one of her attendants, Lady Mary Sidney, helped nurse the queen and caught the disease in the process. She had once been a great beauty but was now disfigured, and had no choice but to withdraw from the court. Queen Elizabeth not only discouraged her from staying, but when Lady Mary paid a visit to court with her husband in 1578 she was not even allocated the standard of lodging that a lady who had almost sacrificed her life for her queen might expect.

➤ Lady Mary Sidney (née Dudley), the gentlewoman attendant of the royal court who nursed Queen Elizabeth through smallpox.

everything from cloth of silver to gold chains for members of the family. Husee was even instructed to scold badly behaved children, and was the kind of totally trustworthy servant that no great family could do without.

There were a few female servants of honour but they had a different role. Even if the head of the household happened to be a woman, a position of responsibility such as steward would be held by a man. A lady might be in charge of her mistress' wardrobe, which would be worth

a great deal of money, especially if her mistress held a position at court, but that was the most she could expect. Her role centred purely on entertaining and caring for her employer.

There was, however, a downside to the life of a servant of honour. Looking good was part of the job, so if ill health struck and took away your good looks it was the end of your career – a fate suffered by one of Elizabeth I's ladies (see panel). Sadly, an ugly attendant, however faithful, was not wanted.

➤ Queen Elizabeth's ladies sit on cushions as their mistress receives Dutch ambassadors, c.1585. Even rich people's houses were not lavishly furnished at this time. Wealth was displayed in fine textiles such as tapestries and carpets as much as in plate and furniture.

THE WORKING DAY

Many Tudors worked as servants when they were young, even if they followed other careers later on. Servants lived in and their employers were responsible for feeding and clothing them, so this worked well for young people. Girls learned the many skills involved in running a house whilst boys learned how to run a farm. It was effectively part of their education.

Servants were paid quarterly rather than weekly, so this was a good way to save for the future if they were self-disciplined. Wages varied a great deal, but in the 1560s an agricultural labourer was paid around 3s 4d (17p) a week. Some servants were paid nothing, just receiving their maintenance. Others received not only money but a variety of extra privileges as well. In 1574–75, an 18-year-old from Essex was hired for 20s (£1) plus the right to pasture two sheep, which would have allowed him to build up a flock as a form of investment.

Both sexes had a great deal to learn. In his *Boke of Husbandrie* (1598), John Fitzherbert explains the housewife's day, which demonstrates the variety of jobs girls had to learn. The day started with sweeping and tidying the house, milking the cows and feeding the calves, then getting the children up. Next came cooking for the family and servants, sending corn and perhaps malt to the miller, feeding the poultry and collecting eggs, making butter and cheese, if it was the right time of year, and feeding the pigs. On top of all this there was the garden to see to, flax, hemp and wool to process, plus dealing with any buying and selling at the market.

A glimpse of the type of men's work expected from servants can be seen from the ploughman's day as recorded by 16th-century English writer Gervase Markham. The work obviously varied depending on the season, but in January Markham tells us that the ploughman would be up around 4 a.m. to go to the stables to feed the horses or oxen (or both) that were used for ploughing, and to clean their stalls. He would then

➤ A 1527 woodcut of a woman churning butter. The profits from the dairy belonged, by tradition, to the woman of the house, but there was hard work involved.

▼ There was not much chance for privacy in Tudor England so it is no surprise that one couple has taken the opportunity for a little romance during haymaking.

groom the animals, water them, then feed them again. Next he would prepare their harness and by around 6 a.m. he would be ready to go in for breakfast. After his meal he would harness the animals and be ploughing by 7 a.m. He would work until 2 or 3 p.m. when he would take the team home to be groomed and fed once more, before being allowed half an hour for his own meal around 4 p.m. After this the ploughman would muck out and feed the team again, then organize their fodder for the next day. It would now be around 6 p.m., and time for supper. Even after supper he would be expected to mend shoes, beat and knock hemp, stamp apples for cider, peel rushes for making rush lights or do other jobs according to the season until 8 p.m. when he went back to the stables to muck out the stalls once more and put litter down for the night. After feeding the animals one last time he was finally free to go to bed.

A servant's lot was not an easy one, but life was not easy for anyone at this level of society and at least they could generally rely on being housed, clothed and fed. Many young people had a better standard of living as servants than when they left to marry and set up their own homes.

◄ *Spring Haymaking*, a 1565 oil painting by Pieter Brueghel the Elder.

➤ In this 1582 engraving, country folk travel to market, whilst fishwives sell pike and an apprentice is sent to fetch water.

Housework took up far more time and required far more energy than it does today. Most cleaning involved water, which was only very rarely piped in. It was often easier to take the work to the water source than the other way round, which meant working outside even in winter. Any indoor facilities that existed were basic. Washing-up, for example, was often done in wooden tubs on a bench. Once a job had been done there was still the problem of getting rid of the dirty water as only the grandest houses had proper drains that allowed it to be poured away. Most people had to take it outside to a sink, which was little more than a hole in the ground. The surrounding plants would eventually soak up the water. Unfortunately this idea did not work in towns where too many sinks in a small area water-logged the ground and killed the plants.

The most basic form of cleaning was scouring and there was a great deal of this to be done.

Most items needed scouring, from knives to anything used in the dairy, such as milk churns. Sharp river sand was usually used, although a plant called horsetail (*Equisetum telmateia*) might be used on anything from pewter plates to armour to bring up the shine. Also known as shavegrass or asprella, it was so widely used that when it became scarce in England in the 18th century it was imported from Holland and became known as Dutch Rushes.

Doing the housework in any house, great or small, included taking measures to deal with vermin. Rats and mice were a problem, just as today, and if your cats let you down then there were professional rat catchers to help out. Perhaps worse, Tudor households also had to deal with a variety of insects from fleas to bedbugs, without the help of modern sprays. Preventing moth-damage to fabric was a particular problem. Woollen clothes were brushed weekly with a soft brush and even

▲ An early 15th-century buttery in Bayleaf Farmhouse at the Weald and Downland Open Air Museum. The buttery (from the word 'butt', a type of barrel) is where items associated with drink were kept and the area would have to be kept very clean.

▲ *Equisetum telmateia*, or 'giant horsetail', a Tudor housewife's cleaning aid. The name comes from the Latin *equus* (horse) and *seta* (bristle).

those in store had to be shaken out regularly to deter the moths. An assortment of substances was used to try to keep them away. Powdered dried orange peel mixed with elecampane root or wormwood and lavender were often used, although one contemporary source commented sadly that they 'small prevayleth'.

▲ *Rhinocoris iracundus*, a member of the bedbug family. These parasitic insects were an unwelcome addition to Tudor living.

Fleas were another menace. One suggestion for catching them was to smear trenchers (slabs of bread used as plates) with glue or turpentine and leave them on the floor at night. A lighted candle was placed in the middle of each, which would attract the fleas and they would stick to the trencher. This was obviously not a method suitable for use with bedding or mattresses, which the fleas particularly loved. Herbs such as wormwood were used to deter them but nothing would rid either a bed or house of them entirely. Bedbugs were an even worse problem. Before settling down to sleep it was usual to search the bed for bugs, although this only helped reduce the numbers rather than solving the problem. Despite the best efforts of the housewife, Tudor life was often far from comfortable.

THE SPREAD OF DISEASE

The link between dirt and disease was well known, and is why Henry VIII ordered his son Edward's rooms to be cleaned daily. No one knew of the existence of bacteria and people thought that disease was caused by bad smells. People did try to keep clean but very few buildings (amongst them Hampton Court) had sewers and proper drains. Most people had little chance of avoiding illness through good hygiene.

▼ *The Royal Nursery* at Hampton Court in 1538, a 19th-century artist's vision. Sadly Prince Edward's apartments at the palace were destroyed by fire.

WASHDAY

All Tudors wore linen underwear, as this was the only fabric that could be easily washed. Poorer people wore strong, thick linen made to last, whilst the wealthy had much finer linen that was bought ready bleached to a brilliant white. This led to the need for 'whiter than white' linen that must have plagued many a housewife. Washing was hard, unpleasant work so it was not surprising that anyone who could afford to paid a laundress to do it for them.

Doing the laundry also meant washing large items like sheets and tablecloths. These had to be folded and placed in a buck tub (similar to a wooden barrel). Sticks were placed between the bundles of linen to allow lye, a strong alkaline solution made with ash, to run freely from top to bottom – a process known as 'lyeing the buck'. The lye was then let out through the tap at the bottom of the tub, then the linen rearranged so it was cleaned evenly. The lye loosened or dissolved dirt, after which the linen was rinsed in running water before being bleached.

◄ This painting entitled *The Boiler* shows a washer-woman adding lye, rather than soap, to wash linen in a buck tub.

► This rather romantic 1582 picture of women doing the laundry disregards the sore hands, aching backs and tiredness caused by Tudor washday.

Metal vats for bleaching only became common in the 17th century. Tudor ones were made from wood, so you could not boil the wash. The bleaching process was therefore similar to 'lyeing the buck'. Human urine was used for making bleach, with public privies sometimes having a special tub for collecting it. The urine was usually added to the lye and must have been very hard on the laundresses' hands.

Soap was also used for doing the washing but its use was confined to delicate fabrics that needed gentle care. At this time laundry soap (known as 'black soap') had the consistency of jelly and had to be stored in a pot or barrel.

Starching was a new skill that the Elizabethan housewife had to learn. This was, of course, essential for maintaining Elizabethan ruffs, but was surprisingly controversial. Starch was often made using grain, and in hard times the rich users of starch were accused of stealing bread from the mouths of the poor. In fact there were other ways of making it. *Gerard's Herbal* of 1597 recommends the use of the plant cuckoopint (*Arum maculatum*), although again this was very hard on the hands of the laundress.

Outer garments were generally made of wool: coarse, heavy wool for the poor and finer, lighter wool for the rich. The wealthiest people's finest clothes were made of luxury fabrics like silk and silk velvet. A single velvet hat bought for one of Elizabeth I's household cost 33s 4d (£1.67)

◄ 'Aping' the fashion, c. 1635. Though a little later than the Tudor period, this satirical engraving shows monkeys – dressed as humans – going through the stages of laundering and starching ruffs.

at a time when agricultural labourers were paid around 3s 4d (17p) a week. Damage to these fine fabrics was a major financial loss so care was needed. As the materials could not be washed they had to be carefully brushed, beaten or shaken. This maintained the look but did not stop them smelling after they had been worn for some time. It was no wonder that the Tudors were so keen on perfumes.

Stains were a major catastrophe. Women's commonplace books (where they wrote useful information) are full of suggestions for removing stains, but there was no easy way of coping. The juice of soapwort (*Saponaria officinalis*) was often used for spot-cleaning. Grease might be removed by using the water in which peas had been cooked, or by applying Castille soap (fine quality toilet soap) with a feather. Another possibility was to use Fuller's Earth, a clay-like substance. If one method did not work, there was always another to try – there was clearly no lack of advice, even if the advice was not always to be relied upon. Certainly maintaining your wardrobe was no easy task in Tudor England.

FASHIONS AND FABRICS

Fabrics were as important as jewellery in demonstrating wealth and social position. They were, of course, hand-woven which made them far more expensive in real terms than modern fabrics, so recycling was the norm at all levels of society. Even in aristocratic families, old clothes were kept and whatever could be salvaged would be reused in new garments.

The time and skill required to weave the finest cloth was considerable. Cloth of gold or silver, for example, required a fine foil of the metal to be cut into thin strips and wrapped around the thread used. This, plus the cost of the metal, made the thread alone so valuable that even Elizabeth I had gold and silver embroidery from her old clothes unpicked and the thread reused.

Tudor attitudes to fashion were different to modern ones. Clothing was yet another badge of rank. In the highest circles, where the fashions were set, impracticality was valued. Most people did some level of manual work so impractical clothes set you above the crowd, making it

impossible to mistake a gentleman for a working man. It also showed that you had servants to help you dress and maintain your wardrobe, and that you had the money to replace your clothes far more frequently than most. The less well-off still copied the fashionable silhouette and cut as far as they could afford, but the effect was rather different.

Colour was also important. The cost of dyes varied enormously. At the cheapest end of the market clothes were often 'white', which meant undyed, so that the wool remained the colour it had been on the sheep. Further up the social scale, country yeomen often chose black for their best clothes as, although the dye was expensive, it lasted and did not show the dirt. Bright colours were more for the conspicuously fashionable and light colours, particularly in silks, were for the very rich as they were extremely hard to keep clean.

Fabrics were, of course, used not only for clothing but also for interior design. Although upholstery did not come into popular use until the 17th century, hangings and cushions were found in great numbers in Tudor homes. Tudor interiors were as bright as their owners could afford. Wall paintings were common, as were painted cloths, both often being painted in imitation of expensive silks or tapestries, a form of decoration favoured by the wealthy. Tapestry was the ultimate luxury. True tapestry is woven rather than embroidered; it has to be made by skilled weavers and in Tudor times the designs could be commissioned from the most famous artists. Raphael designed one particular set of tapestries for Pope Leo X to hang in the Sistine Chapel in Rome. Such items were so valuable that they were very carefully treated. The dyes – particularly the bright ones –

▼ Typical 16th-century fashions, as worn by the wealthy.

▲ Detail of a woman spinning, from a wool and silk tapestry, c. 1500. Most girls were taught to spin in Tudor times.

◄ The High Great Chamber, Hardwick Hall. Bess of Hardwick, determined to impress, has all the symbols of wealth on display. The tapestries have faded over the years but the colours would have been very strong when new.

faded quickly, so were kept out of the light as much as possible. The finest hangings, even in royal circles, were kept rolled up in the dark and brought out only on occasions when their owners particularly wanted to impress. The aristocracy needed their fine fabrics to demonstrate their wealth and power as much as they needed their great houses.

TUDOR SPLENDOUR

This 1595 painting of Lady Eleanor Percy hangs in Powis Castle in Wales. Her elaborate style conforms to the popular view of how the Tudors dressed, although in fact only a tiny section of the population could afford such luxury. Portraits like this were often commissioned to celebrate important events, such as a marriage or a court promotion, and subjects were often painted wearing the splendid garments associated with the occasion, making the clothes exceptional even in the highest circles.

◄ Lady Eleanor Percy.

FEEDING THE HOUSEHOLD

Bread, of which there was a great variety, was the most important food in Tudor England. The finest quality bread, manchet, was white. This was luxury bread for the rich as the flour had to be sifted through a cloth to remove the bran. The next grade down was brown bread, made with wheat flour, but loaves were also made from other grains, such as barley, or from a mixture of grains. There was even bread made from dried peas, but this was usually intended for horses.

The other necessity of life was pottage, which was anything edible that could be made into a thick soup. Beans, peas, any vegetables the household had to hand, all went in. It was easy to make and very convenient as it could be left to cook over the fire for hours. If you were fortunate, the pottage also contained meat, but lower down in society it was rare to eat meat every day. If you had meat it was likely to be pork, as pigs were easy to keep.

The higher you were in society, the more meat would appear at mealtimes, with hunted fare being more prestigious than farmed. Wealthy houses might also be able to provide food from a dovecote or fish pond (fish being eaten on days when the Church forbade meat). In well-to-do houses a variety of different dishes would appear on the table at the same time, using various meats or fish of the season. If hosts wanted to impress their guests, they also needed to include expensive imported luxuries such as sugar, spices or citrus fruit in their meals.

Food for everyone, rich or poor, was more expensive than it is today in comparative terms, not just in England but all over Europe. At the end of the 16th century, even in the rich city of Antwerp in Belgium about four-fifths of the

▼ In this 1602 painting a family is portrayed saying grace at a table laden with food, including meat, and luxurious tableware, such as drinking glasses.

▲ Bread ovens were heated by building a fire inside. Once the bread was baked, the remaining heat was used to cook items needing a gentler temperature.

average income went on food. This meant food was very acceptable as a gift, even in the highest circles. When John Petre, son of Sir William Petre (who built Ingatestone Hall – see page 5), was christened, one friend sent a guinea fowl, a mallard, a woodcock, two teals, a basket of wafers and a variety of cakes for the christening feast.

Consumable gifts were particularly welcome on great occasions as preparing a large feast in the days before refrigeration was a challenge. Food could be preserved in a variety of ways, such as salting or drying, for the longer term but trying to keep fresh food in an edible condition was more difficult. A thick pie crust could be used to preserve cooked meat as it kept out the air, but generally the only alternative was to kill the animals to be eaten as late as possible before they were needed and to do all the preparation work at the last minute. Preparing for a royal visit must have been particularly difficult. Lord Keeper Edgerton spent about £240 on food when he entertained Elizabeth I for four days at

Harefield Place, north-west of London, in 1602. Given that Queen Elizabeth often changed her itinerary at the last minute, the cost and trouble to her courtiers of these changes of heart must have been considerable, resulting in a great deal of expensive waste. Worse still, if the queen made an unexpected visit at short notice, obtaining and preparing enough food was not easy. Fortunately it was only the very great who were expected to feed and entertain the whole royal court. A country gentleman who had his house commandeered for the royal progress was only expected to move out and leave it clean and ready for use. There were some compensations for not moving in the highest of circles.

➤ Pepper was an expensive luxury in Tudor times. This pepper mill was found on the *Mary Rose*, a favourite ship of Henry VIII that was sunk in battle in 1545 but is now displayed in Portsmouth Historic Dockyard.

DIET AND HEALTH

There was an interest in healthy eating in the 16th century and several books were published on the subject, though their authors had rather different opinions to those held today. These authors were university-trained doctors, or were influenced by them, and by no means everyone who practised medicine at the time came from this background. Doctors charged high fees and only the rich could afford them. Further down the social scale came the barber-surgeons who practised surgery and were called in where bloodletting was thought helpful. Apothecaries, like modern pharmacists, made up prescriptions for doctors but could be consulted directly. Everyday illnesses were treated by the woman of the house who would be brought up to have a knowledge of herbal medicines. The result of this demarcation was that doctors had a knowledge that was theoretical rather than practical.

Dissecting dead bodies and the study of detailed anatomy was just starting to become part of a doctor's training, but at this time medical studies were dominated by astrology and the theory of the four humours. People had long been aware of the moon's influence on the tides and it was presumed that the stars influenced the humours of the body in the same way. The four humours that were believed to make up all things were: fire (hot), air (cold), water (moist) and earth (dry). In addition, there were four basic character types: sanguine (hot and moist), phlegmatic (cold and moist), choleric (hot and dry) and melancholic (cold and dry). To eat healthily you needed to not only understand the humours and the type of character that you were, but also the nature of the food you planned to eat. For example, garlic, onion,

leek and mustard were thought to encourage choler (anger), whilst white salt fish encouraged melancholy. This was further complicated by the fact that the nature of vegetables was considered to change according to the season; the same theory was applied to meat, the make-up of which was also said to change depending on the age of the animal. Even the time of day something was eaten could alter its qualities: a proverb of the day stated 'Butter is gold in the morning, silver at noon and lead at night'.

So although the ideas behind 'healthy' eating were fairly simple, in practice anyone who was serious about it needed the (expensive) advice of a professional – and, as in any age, even the experts could not agree. For example, Andrew Boorde, physician to Henry VIII, considered cream a bad thing, whilst Thomas Cogan, another 16th-century physician, praised it; the

➤ Zodiac Man. This type of illustration, found in medical books, demonstrated which signs of the zodiac were thought to dominate specific parts of the body. This image is from *The Guild Book of the Barber Surgeons of York*, published in 1486.

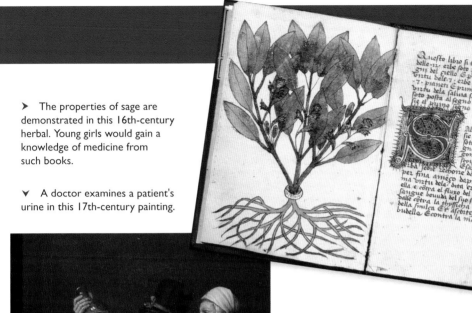

> The properties of sage are demonstrated in this 16th-century herbal. Young girls would gain a knowledge of medicine from such books.

∨ A doctor examines a patient's urine in this 17th-century painting.

the Dutch, who were used to it, but harmful to the English, whom he thought should drink ale (brewed without hops). The idea that everyone's body, whether rich or poor, English or foreign, worked in the same way was not something that came naturally to 16th-century minds.

One piece of good news was that the idea of healthy eating was only a problem for a small section of society. Most people could only afford what was available locally, whether it was considered healthy or not. At least that was one less thing to worry about.

early-Greek philosopher and pharmacist Galen approved of pork, whilst Boorde considered it to be unhealthy.

Social background was another consideration when it came to diet. It was generally assumed that one class of person could eat things that another would find harmful, simply because they were not used to eating that particular thing. Cogan considered brown bread and butter a good breakfast for country people, whilst expensive white bread was recommended for the genteelly bred. Andrew Boorde believed beer (brewed with hops) to be a healthy drink for

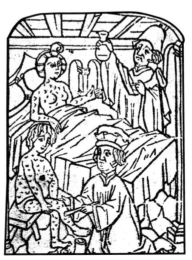

◄ Physicians treat a couple suffering from syphilis in this 15th-century illustration.

WHAT'S COOKING?

Tudor cooks worked with very basic facilities. Many people had only one fire for both heat and cooking; it was a wealthy kitchen indeed that had more than one fireplace and the middle-class housewife could find her facilities stretched when entertaining.

Most Tudor houses had a central hearth or a more modern wall-mounted fireplace with a chimney above. If you were lucky enough to have a chimney, you could have permanent fixtures to help you cook, such as metal pothooks fixed to the wall which would take the weight of a cauldron, and which would allow you to adjust the height of the cooking pot above the fire.

Cooking over an open fire was quite a skill, with different levels of heat required for different types of cooking. The cook often needed one end of the fire to be blazing hot, whilst the other end had to be cooler. For anything requiring gentle heat there were metal dishes called posnets, which had three legs and stood amongst the embers. In wealthy people's kitchens there were often charcoal stoves (a little like a modern barbecue), as charcoal could provide a gentle, constant heat which was good for making sauces or delicate confectionery work.

Kitchen equipment needed to be kept simple to save space, though in any case all most could afford were the basics. A large pot to go over the fire in which to cook pottage or boil a piece of meat was the absolute necessity. Bread was more of a problem. Bread ovens took up space and were expensive to heat, so many houses did not have one. If there was a local baker you could, of course, buy loaves from him, or pay to use his oven. If that was not possible, dough could be

▲ Pewter tableware rescued from the wreck of the *Mary Rose*. When it was polished pewter looked very like silver, so it was a popular choice.

▲ Food is prepared before an enormous fireplace in this reconstruction of a Tudor kitchen at Kentwell Hall, Suffolk. Kitchens were hot places to work and spitboys in royal kitchens had to be told not to work naked.

baked under a metal pot, or some forms of bread could be cooked on a hot stone.

Large pieces of meat were roasted in front of fires on metal spits. Turning the spit was especially unpleasant as there was not only the heat from the fire to contend with but also the cold draught from the air that roared up the chimney. In 1536, royal physician Dr John Cauis described a turnspit dog – a little dog trained to run inside a treadmill which powered the spit via a pulley. Mechanical jacks for turning the spit existed at this time but only really became common in the 18th century.

Not everyone had to worry about turning the spit. Smaller pieces of meat, which is all many people were ever likely to have, could be suspended from a hook on a skein of worsted. The thread would be twisted tightly so that it gradually unwound, thus turning the meat in front of the fire and cooking it. Tudor cooks were seemingly very resourceful.

◀ A 16th-century kitchen at work. Note the pot on the hook over the fire where the spit is being loaded, and the diners waiting in the next room.

A FEAST ON A SPIT

Gervase Markham, in his book *The English Huswife, Containing the Inward and Outward Virtues Which Ought to Be in a Complete Woman,* explained how to cook a chine of beef, a loin of mutton, a capon and a lark at the same time. The beef, the largest item, had to be parboiled until half cooked. The capon was put on the spit next to the hand of the person turning it (who would stand at the cooler end of the fire). The beef went beside the capon and then finally the mutton was added. The beef and the fat part of the mutton covered the lark, so that it cooked very slowly. The capon and mutton were basted with cold water and salt to slow their cooking time, whilst the beef was basted with boiling lard to make it cook faster. When the beef was almost done, the mutton and capon were basted with butter until everything was ready to be served at the same time.

THE ETIQUETTE OF DINING

Good table manners were essential to the well-bred Tudor. They did not use the word 'etiquette', though; they used the word 'courtesy', and the idea was that everything you did or said demonstrated your elegant upbringing, consideration for others and respect for God. Table manners were simply part of courtesy. Courtesy manuals, however, were written for the wealthy – how far down society these rules were followed is questionable.

To understand Tudor manners it is necessary to consider how they ate. Forks were not yet in general use for dining, and in most cases diners were even expected to bring their own knife and spoon to the table. Most people carried these items with them all the time, and spoons in particular were often valued personal items, which is why it was common to give a child a spoon as a christening gift. Although private dining in small dining rooms was becoming fashionable, at large formal feasts even noble people ate at trestle tables that were assembled for meal times and taken down afterwards. The tabletops were often warped and not fastened to the trestles, so leaning an elbow on the table could make the whole thing wobble.

Given that diners were on display at table, it was important to be clean and neat when eating. It was bad manners to spill food on either one's clothes or the white linen tablecloth. To keep clean, extensive use was made of table napkins. These were longer than modern napkins and were placed over the left shoulder or wrist. The Tudors ate with their right hand only, taking care not to allow any sauce to go beyond the first knuckle of the fingers, which were then wiped on a napkin.

Many of the rules for polite dining were concerned with sharing communal bowls and plates. It was common for diners to share a 'mess', a portion of food usually meant for four diners, with two sitting at one side of a trestle table and two at the other. When eating from a communal bowl it was rude to leave your spoon in the dish as it made it harder for the other diners to dip in. Equally, if you were sharing a piece of meat, it was not the done thing to pick it up and bite a portion off. Instead, you would cut a morsel off the communal meat and put it on your plate. There may well have been sauce on the table, in little bowls (known as saucers), into which meat was dipped before being placed in the mouth. Anything a diner did not want to eat went into a large dish called a voider, and certainly not back in the communal dish.

◄ Sir Henry Unton (c. 1557–96) dines at his wedding feast in this detail from a painting in the National Portrait Gallery, London. Note the napkins folded and placed over the shoulders of some guests.

Table manners were also designed to remind everyone of their social place. Seating was arranged according to rank and when sharing dishes the most important person of the group served themselves first. The more important you were, the fewer people you shared with, so that higher-ranking diners ate two to a mess rather than four. The most important diners did not share at all.

Despite the delicacy of 16th-century manners, some things were permitted that would shock the modern diner. For example, spitting was allowed, although it was done discreetly. And if they had to blow their noses, people were advised to wipe their hands on their clothes so that others did not have to see the result. Tudor dining was not always as elegant as it might have been.

➤ This rock crystal tableware, which belonged to William Cecil, 1st Baron Burghley, shows the lavish nature of feasting in court circles. These magnificent items can be seen in Hatfield House, Hertfordshire, which has been home to the Cecil family since it was built by William Cecil's son, Robert, in 1611.

⌄ This heavily embossed silver-gilt ewer and basin, dating from c. 1546, is held in the British Museum, London. Elaborately decorated items like these were available for house guests to wash their hands.

FEASTS AND BANQUETS

A feast and a banquet were not necessarily the same thing in Tudor times. A feast was a large meal, whilst a banquet could also mean a small private meal, generally for intimate friends.

Banquets originated with the habit of serving sweet luxuries such as wafers and spiced wine to the more important guests at the end of a meal. As the tables were usually being cleared away at this time to allow entertainment to take place, the guests would withdraw to a private room. Gradually this evolved so that guests withdrew to special banquet houses. These were often designed to have beautiful views, so many were built on the roofs of grand houses. To provide a fit setting, the banquet houses themselves were as original and beautiful as possible. The finest sweet luxuries would be served; even the cups and plates used could be specially made of sugar paste so that they could be eaten at the end of the meal. Alternatively, the plates might be made of painted wood and elaborately decorated with verses that could be sung or said by the guests as a game. These occasions were intended to be very intimate, providing an opportunity for even the greatest of men and women to relax and enjoy their friends' company, so any unnecessary servants would withdraw.

Moral opinion was divided over banquets as sugar was considered an aphrodisiac. Many of the sweetmeats associated with banquets had such names as 'kissing comfits', so it was not surprising that these very private occasions were often associated with unseemly behaviour.

A feast was a much larger entertainment than a banquet and often came with political overtones, particularly in court circles. A feast's most obvious use was as a display of wealth and therefore power, with the host overwhelming guests with lavish hospitality. The food, however, was only part of the entertainment.

Guests invited to a courtly feast might come away richer. It was common for courtiers to take part in the entertainments and the costumes worn were made of the finest materials, particularly cloth of gold which looked spectacular by candlelight. It was important for hosts to demonstrate their liberality on these occasions, so participants were often allowed to keep their costumes. Those not taking part were

◄ Food is brought in and wine is poured by servants at a 16th-century courtly feast – although the food does not appear to be the main interest of those seated round the table on this occasion.

➤ One of the tent designs for the Field of Cloth of Gold, 1520. Every detail for this important meeting between the English and French kings was carefully planned. This design demonstrates the sheer opulence of the occasion.

▲ Hans Holbein's depiction of musicians at the court of Henry VIII in Whitehall Palace in London. Music was an important part of court entertainment and the king showed a great personal interest in his musical household.

▲ Stone table in the Upper Room of Sharington's Tower at Lacock Abbey, Wiltshire. This table, carved with Greek gods and goddesses, was built for banquets and would have been laden with food and choice wine whilst guests admired the view from the windows.

sometimes allowed to take elements of the costumes, or even scenery. In 1511, Henry VIII was taking part in an entertainment where the costumes were covered in golden ornaments. The Spanish ambassadors had prior permission to remove some of these decorations during the entertainment but, when they did so, the rest of the audience took this to mean that anyone could have them. This resulted in the participants, including the king himself, being stripped not only of their gold ornaments but also of their clothes! Court entertainments were not always dignified.

THE MEANING OF MOUNTAINS

The Tudors were adept at symbolism and there could be political overtones to everything at a feast, from the theme of the masques which followed dinner to the choice of clothing. At the Field of Cloth of Gold, the great meeting between Henry VIII and Francis I of France in 1520, one of King Henry's costumes was covered in small mountains, from which sprung branches of basil made of gold. In *Hall's Chronicle* of 1542, the author Edward Hall records how a mountain represented England and was a warning to the French not to damage the 'sweet herbs' of England.

BEER, ALE AND WINE

There was very little choice of beverages in the 16th century and most were alcoholic. Water was not safe to drink and milk was a precious resource for making cheese or butter, so the whey left over from cheese-making was all that tended to be drunk. Tea, coffee and chocolate were not imported until the 17th century. Wine was too expensive for most, so that left beer as the normal daily drink. The ability to brew beer was as important a skill for women as the ability to bake bread. Many professional brewers were female as it was one of the few ways in which widows or single women could earn a living.

Today we tend to use the words 'beer' and 'ale' to mean the same thing but this was not generally the case in the 16th century. Both were brewed from barley, but hops were added to beer and not to ale. To confuse matters, some stronger beers were referred to as ales.

Hops were added to beer not only for flavour but also because they acted as a preservative, which was incredibly important. As beer lasted longer, it could be brewed in larger quantities and less often than ale (made without hops) which could go off very easily, especially in hot weather. The use of hops was introduced from Flanders in the late 15th century and was not without controversy, as in some quarters beer was considered unhealthy for the English. Despite this, in southern England the change to beer was complete by the end of the 16th century. In northern England it was too cold to grow hops which made them expensive and hard to obtain, so the change took longer.

There were various types of beer. William Harrison commented that noblemen drank beer that had been aged for one or even two years,

but that general household beer for most was only about a month old. There were also beers of different strengths. Brewers generally used the malt three times. The brew got weaker with use so that the third brew produced what was known as 'small beer'. This was very weak and bitter and was considered by brewers to be a bonus which paid for the fuel for the brewing. It did not keep and was a cheap drink given most commonly to the lower members of the household. In many houses the stronger beers were kept under lock and key, but there was free access to the small beer.

Given the amount of alcohol consumed it is not surprising that there seems to have been a relaxed attitude towards drunkenness. Drinking was a vital part of social events, when proposing toasts to members of the company was the norm.

➤ Men at work in a brewery, c. 1550. Large-scale brewing became more common as the use of hops meant that the beer lasted longer.

> ➤ This beautiful blue and white tankard, made of Venetian glass c. 1548, is held in the British Museum; such a luxury item would have been owned by a wealthy person.

> ➤ Most Tudors drank from wooden tankards. This one was found on the *Mary Rose*.

People did not respond to a toast by taking a polite sip as happens today, but instead were expected to drain the entire glass. To refuse to drink a toast, or to fail to drain the glass, was considered extremely bad manners.

However, the reliance on beer was by no means all bad. The calories in it were a help at a time when most people led very active lives. Beer also contained all the main nutrients, except fat, that people needed and was an important source of vitamin B. In addition, the price of beer rose more slowly than the price of food, making it a central part of the Tudor diet and more than a drink.

WINE, THE GENTLEMAN'S DRINK

Wine was *the* drink for a Tudor gentleman. Being imported, it was much more expensive than beer. Charges on wine, once it had arrived in England, included lighterage (to take the wine from the ship to shore), cranage (use of a crane for unloading) and cooperage (cost of barrels) even before import duties had been paid. In the homes of the Earl and Countess of Northumberland, a country seat at Petworth House in West Sussex and Syon House on the outskirts of London, the lord and lady of the house drank wine regularly but its issue to anyone else in the household was closely monitored. The wine cellar in any house was kept under lock and key, but in a society that was obsessed by social position, anyone who wished to be considered as 'someone' had to not only drink wine themselves but also to offer it to their guests.

PLACES TO VISIT

A number of Tudor buildings, or those with Tudor links, survive today and a selection of those well worth a visit are given below. Although the interiors of many are so changed there is little sense left of what they were like to live in during Tudor times, several of those listed here have some fine examples of their original interiors. It is always harder, however, to find places that reflect the lives of ordinary people rather than the rich, but two that achieve this particularly well are the Weald and Downland Open Air Museum and Alfriston Clergy House, details of which are also given below.

Athelhampton House, Athelhampton, Dorchester, Dorset DT2 7LG; 01305 848363; www.athelhampton.co.uk

Burghley House, Stamford, Lincolnshire PE9 3JY; 01780 752451; www.burghley.co.uk

Dorney Court, Windsor, Berkshire SL4 6QP; 01628 604638; www.dorneycourt.co.uk

Gwydir Castle, Llanrwst, Conwy LL26 0PN; 01492 641687; www.gwydircastle.co.uk

Haddon Hall, Bakewell, Derbyshire DE45 1LA; 01629 812855; www.haddonhall.co.uk

Hampton Court Palace, East Molesey, Surrey KT8 9AU; 0844 482 7777; www.hrp.org.uk/hamptoncourtpalace

Hatfield House, Hatfield Park, Great North Road, Hatfield, Hertfordshire AL9 5NQ; 01707 287010; www.hatfield-house.co.uk

Hever Castle, Hever, Near Edenbridge, Kent TN8 7NG; 01732 865224; www.hevercastle.co.uk

Kelmscott Manor, Kelmscott, Lechlade, Gloucestershire GL7 3HJ; 01367 252486; www.kelmscottmanor.co.uk

Kentwell Hall, Long Melford, Suffolk CO10 9BA; 01787 310207; www.kentwell.co.uk

Leeds Castle, nr Maidstone, Kent ME17 1PL; 01622 765400; www.leeds-castle.com

Longleat House, Longleat, Warminster, Wiltshire BA12 7NW; 01985 844328; www.longleat.co.uk/explore/longleat-house

Plas Mawr, High Street, Conwy LL32 8DE; 01492 580167; www.cadw.wales.gov.uk

Shakespeare's Birthplace, Henley Street, Stratford-upon-Avon, Warwickshire CV37 6QW; 01789 204 016; http://houses.shakespeare.org.uk (for this and other Shakespeare Birthplace Trust Houses)

Stanley Palace, Watergate Street, Chester, Cheshire CH1 2LF; 01244 325586; www.stanleypalace.com

St Fagans Castle, St Fagans National History Museum, Cardiff, Glamorgan CF5 6XB; 029 2057 3500; www.museumwales.ac.uk/en/stfagans

Sudeley Castle, Winchcombe, Gloucestershire GL54 5JD; 01242 602308; www.sudeleycastle.co.uk

Temple Newsam, Temple Newsam Road, Leeds LS15 0AE; 0113 264 7321; www.leeds.gov.uk/templenewsamhouse

Weald and Downland Open Air Museum, Chichester, West Sussex PO18 0EU; 01243 811348; www.wealddown.co.uk

Wilton House, Wilton, Salisbury, Wiltshire SP2 0BJ; 01722 746700; www.wiltonhouse.com

ENGLISH HERITAGE

Contact details for all English Heritage properties: 0870 333 1181; www.english-heritage.org.uk

Bayham Abbey, Clay Hill Road, Lamberhurst, Kent TN3 8AX

Eltham Palace, Court Yard, Eltham, Greenwich, London SE9 5QE

Kenilworth Castle, Castle Green, Kenilworth, Warwickshire CV8 1NE

National Trust

Website for all National Trust properties: www.nationaltrust.org.uk

Alfriston Clergy House, The Tye, Alfriston, East Sussex BN26 5TL; 01323 870001

Buckland Abbey, Yelverton, Devon PL20 6EY; 01822 853607

Cotehele, St Dominick, near Saltash, Cornwall PL12 6TA; 01579 351346

Hardwick Hall, Doe Lea, Chesterfield, Derbyshire S44 5QJ; 01246 850430

Ightham Mote, Ivy Hatch, Sevenoaks, Kent TN15 0NT; 01732 810378

Lacock Abbey, Lacock, near Chippenham, Wiltshire SN15 2LG; 01249 730459

Little Moreton Hall, Congleton, Cheshire CW12 4SD; 01260 272018

Montacute House, Montacute, Somerset TA15 6XP; 01935 823289

Paycocke's, 25 West Street, Coggeshall, Colchester, Essex C06 1NS; 01376 561305

Rufford Old Hall, 200 Liverpool Road, Rufford, near Ormskirk, Lancashire L40 1SG; 01704 821254

Speke Hall, The Walk, Liverpool L24 1XD; 0844 800 4799

Trerice, Kestle Mill, near Newquay, Cornwall TR9 4PG; 01637 875404

Tudor Merchant's House, Quay Hill, Tenby, Pembrokeshire SA70 7BX; 01834 842279

The Vyne, Vyne Road, Sherborne St John, Basingstoke, Hampshire RG24 9HL; 01256 883858

Information correct at time of going to press.

BACKGROUND: Hever Castle in Kent.